MALACHY

RICHARD JOHNSON

Printed in the United States of America
ISBN 978-1-958434-38-3 (sc)
ISBN 978-1-958434-39-0 (e)

2022.06.16

MainSpring Books
5901 W. Century Blvd
Suite 750
Los Angeles, CA, US, 90045

www.mainspringbooks.com

Malachy

chapter 1

1. Al Massa al dabar Al Yachuwshauh al Yashara Al arach Malachy 2. any hayach ahab attah amar
Al Yachuwshauh ad attah amar Mah yash ahab anachnw hayach lah rasha yaaqab ah amar
Al Yachuwshauh ad any ahab yaaqab 3. av any sana Asa av shuwm Naphash har av Naphash Nachalah
shamamah al tannah al Madbar ky 4. ky Adam amar any huw Rashash han any ahy shwb av banah
charbah Maqam kah amar Al Yachuwshauh Al Tsaba cham yash banah han ahy harac av cham yash
qara cham gabal al Rashah av am al Asar Al Yachuwshauh hayach zaam Alam 5. av Naphash ayn
yash raah av yash amar Al Yachuwshauh ahy huw gabal al gabal Al YasharaAl 6. ban kabad
Naphash ab av abad Naphash adan am az any huw ab ayach huw any kabad av am any huw Adan
ayach huw any Mara amar Al Yachuwshauh Al Tsaba al attah la kahan ky bazah any sham av
7. attah Nagash gaal lacham al any Mazbaach av attah amar Mah hayach any gaal attah al ky attah
amar al shalchan Al Yachuwshauh huw bazah 8. ky attah Nagash avvar al zabach huw yash lah Ra
av ky attah Nagash al paccaach av chalah huw yash lah Ra qarab yash Na al attah pachah ahy huw
ratsah ad attah aw Nasa attah panym amar Al Yachuwshauh Al Tsaba 9. aw attah Na chalah Al ky huw
ahy chanan ashar anachnw zath hayach arach Naphash yad Ahy Nasa Naphash panym amar
Al Yachuwshauh Al Tsaba 10.Mah huw sham gam al attah ky Tsaba cagar dalath al channam lah
asah attah Ar ash Mazbaach al channam any hayach lah chaphats al attah amar Al Yachuwshauh
Al Tsaba lah ahy ratsah achad Manchah al Naphash yad. 11. yth al Mazrach al shamash gam al al
Mabw al huw any sham yash gadal al Gowy aw al kal Maqam qatsar yash Nagash al any sham
aw tahar Machah al any sham yash gadal al Gowy amar Al YachuwshauhAl Tsaba12. han huw hayach
chalal yash al ky attah amar al shalchan Al Yachuwshauh huw qaal aw al Nayb sham gam Naphash
attah amar gam hannah Mah Matta laah huw yash av attah akal huw bazah 13 hayach Naphach al
al yash amar Al Yachuwshauh Al Tsaba av attah huw ky hayach gazal av paccaach av chalah kah
Manchah yash ratsah zath al Naphash yad amar Al Yachuwshauh attah bow al Raa Manchah yash
ratsah 14. han arar al Nakal yash al Naphash adar zakar av Nadar av zabach al Al Yachuwshauh
shachath dabar al any hayach gadal Malak amar Al Yachuwshauh Al Tsaba av any sham huw
yara Al Gowy.

chapter 2

1. aw attah la attah kahan zath Matsavah huw al attah 2. am attah ahy alah shama aw am attah ahy Lah shama aw am attah ahy Lah shuwm yash Lah Nathan kabad al any sham amar Al Yachuwshauh Al Tsaba ahy gam shalach Maarah al attah aw ahy arar Naphash Barakah gam any hayach arar cham kabar ky attah asah Lah suwm Lab 3. han ahy gaar Naphash zara aw zarah parash al Naphash panym gam parash al Naphash chag aw kash yash Nasa attah cuwr ad yash 4. aw attah yash yada ky any hayach shalach zath Matsavah al attah ky any barayth chayl kal zath Lavay amar Al Yachuwshauh Al Tsaba 5. any Barayth hayach han Naphash al chay aw shalam aw Nathan cham al Naphash yth al Mara ashar huw yara any aw hayach chathath panym Naphash sham 6. Al Tarah al amath hayach al Naphash pah aw aval hayach Lah Matsa al Naphash saphah huw halak han any al shalam aw Mayshar aw asah shuwb rab cuwr al avan 7. al ky kahan saphah yash Shamar daath aw cham yash baqash al tarah Al Naphash pah al huw al Mala ha Al Yachuwshauh Al tsaba 8. han attah cuwr ha al darak attah hayach Nathan Rab al kash al Tarah attah hayach shachath barayth ha Lavay amar Al yachuwshauh Al Tsaba 9. al hayach any gam Nathan attah bazah aw shaphal panym kal al am pah huw attah hayach lah Shamar any darak han hayach Nasa al Al Tarah 10. hayach anachnw lah kal achad Ab yash lah achad Al bara anachnw Madda asah any asah bagad kal kash al Naphash ach arach chalal Al Barayth al Anachnw Ab 11. Yachadah yash asah bagad aw ach Tabah huw asah al YasharaAl aw al shalam al yachadah yash chalal al qadash ha Al Yachuwshauh Asar huw ahab aw yash baal al bath al Nakar Al 12. Yachwshauh ahy karath al kash ky asah zath al uwr aw ky anah al Ahal ha al yaaqab aw Naphash ky Nagash Manchah al Al Yachuwshauh Al Tsaba 13. aw zath hayach attah asah shany kacah al Mazbaach ha Al Yachuwshauh han damah han bakay aw han anaqah bayth ky huw panah lah al Manchah kash ad aw laqach han ratsan ahay al Naphash yad14. ad attah amar al Al Yachuwshauh yash hayach ad bayn attah aw kashshah al attah Naar al Asar yash asah baqad ad huw Naphash attah chabarath aw kashshah al attah Barayth 15. aw asah lah huw asah achad ad hayach huw al shaar al al ruwach aw Mah achad ky huw chayl baqash Alasham zara kan Nasa shamar al Naphash ruwach aw yanach al asah bagad al kashshah al Naphash Naar 16. yth Al Yachuwshauh Al Alasham Al YasharaAl amar ky huw sana shalach cuwr al achad kacah ach han Naphash labash amar Al Yachuwshauh Al Tsaba kan Nasa shamar al Naphash ruwach ky attah asah lah bagad 17. attah hayach yaga Al Yachuwshauh han Naphash dabar ad attah amar Mah hayach any yaga Naphash yowm attah amar kal achad ky asah ra huw tabal al ayn Al Yachwshauh aw huw chaphats al cham aw ayach huw Al Alasham al Mashpat.

chapter 3

han ahy shalach any Malak aw yash panah al darak panym any aw Al Yachuwshauh Asar allah baqash yash patham bow al Naphash haykal gam al Malak al Barayth Asar attah chaphats al hannah yash bow amar Al Yachuwshauh Al Tsaba 2. han My wlay kowl al yowm al Naphash bow aw My yash amad yowm huw raah al huw kamw tsaraph ash aw kamw kabac Barayth 3.av yash yashab huw Tsaraph aw tahar al kacaph aw huw yash tahar al ban al lavay aw zaqaq cham huw zahab aw kacaph ky cham wlay Nagash al Al Yachuwshauh Manchah al Tsadaqah 4. az yash al Manchah al yachadah aw shalam arah al Al Yachuwshauh huw al yowm al Alam aw al qadmany shanah 5. aw ahy qarab attah Mashpst aw ahy Mahar ad al al kashaph aw al al Naaph aw al shaqar shaba aw al cham ky ashaq al Sakyr al Naphash sakar al almanah al yathamaw ky Natah al gar al Naphash yamyn aw yara lah any amar Al Yachuwshah Al Tsaba 6. al hayach Al Yachuwshauh any shanah lah kan attah ban al yaaqab huw lah kalah 7. gam al al yowm al Naphash Ab attah huw cowr al any chaq aw hayach lah shamar cham showb al any aw ahy showb al attah amar Al Yachuwshauh Al Tsaba han attah amar Mah   yash any showb 8.ahy adam qaba Alasham ad attah hayach qaba any han attah amar Mah hayach any qaba attah al Maasar aw Taramah 9. attah arar han Maarah al attah hayach qaba any gam zath kal gay 10. bow attah kal al Maasar al al wtsar ky sham wlay huw taraph al any bayth aw bachan any Na zath amar Al Yachuwshauh Al Tsaba am ahy lah pathach attah al arabbah al shamaym aw shachaph attah barakah sham yash lah rachab day laqach yash 11.aw ahy gaar al akal al Naphash dabrah aw huw yash lah shachath al paray al Naphash adamah lah yash Naphash gaphan shahal Naphash sakal panym Al ath al sadah amar Al Yachuwshauh Al Tsaba 12. aw kal gay yash Asar attah Asar al yash chaphat arats amar Al Yachuwshauh Tsaba 13. Naphash dabar hayach chazaq al any amar Al Yachuwshauh ad attah amar Mah hayach any dabar kan rabah al attah 14. attah hayach amar yash shav abad Alasham aw Mah batsa yash ky any hayach shamar Naphash Mashmarath ky any hayach halak qadarannyth panym Al Yachuwshauh Al Tsaba 15. aw attah any ashar al zad shalah gam cham ky asah rashah huw banah gam cham ky bachan Alasham huw gam Malat 16. az cham ky yara Al Yachuwshauh dabar day achad Alraa aw Al Yachuwshauh qashab aw shama aw caphar Al zakar hayach kathab panym Naphash al cham ky yara Al Yachuwshauh aw ky chashab al Naphash sham 17. aw cham yash any amar Al Yachuwshauh al Tsaba al ky yowm Asar any asah al any cagallah aw ahy chamal cham huw kash chamal Naphash ratsan ban ky abad Naphash 18. az yash showb aw raah bayn al Tsaddyq aw al rasha bayn Naphash ky abad Alasham aw Naphash ky abad Naphash lah.

chapter 4

1. al hannah al yowm bow ky yash baar huw tannar aw kal al zad gam aw kal ky asah rashah yash qash aw al yowm ky bow yash lahat cham amar Al Yachuwshauh Al Tsaba ky yash azab cham lah sharash aw anaph 2. han al attah ky yara any sham yash al shamash al Tsadaqah zarach han Marpa al Naphash kanaph aw yash yatsa aw pash huw agal al al Marbaq 3. aw yash acac al rasha al cham yash aphar tachath al kaph al Naphash ragal al yowm ky yash asah zath amar Al Yachuwshauh Al Tsaba 4. zakar attah Al Tarah Al Mashash any abad Asar any tsavah al Naphash al charab al kal yasharaAl han al chaq aw Mashpat 5. hannah ahy shalach attah Alayachuw al Naby panym al bow al gadal Al Yachuwshauh 6. aw yash shuwb al lab al Ab al ban aw al lab al al ban al cham ab pan any bow awNakah al arats han charam.

ᴋ ᴋ	Aleph aw-Lef
ᴄ ᴄ	Beyth
ᴅ ᴅ	Daleth daw-leth
ᴎ ᴎ	he hay
ᴵ ᴵ ᴵ	Vav
ᴵ ᴵ	Zayin
ᴎ	Chevth
ᴵ ᴵ	Yowde
ᴵ ᴵ	Kaph caf
ᴵ ᴵ	Lamed Law med
ᴵ ☐	Mem mame
ᴵ	NuwN Noon
▽ ▽	Camek Saw mck
ᴦ ᴦ	AYiN ah-YiN
ᴵ ᴵ	phe fay
ᴵ	Tsadev
ᴵ	Qowph cofe
ᴵ	Revsh
ᴵ ᴵ	shivn sheen
ᴵ ᴵ	Thav

chapter 1

Massa al dabar Al Yachuwshauh
al yasharaAl arach Malachy .
Any hayach ahab attah
amar Al Yachuwshauh ad
attah amar Mah
yash ahab anachnw
hayach lah asha yaaqab
 ah amar al Yachuwshauh
ad any ahab yaaaqab
aw any sana rasha
aw showm Naphash har
aw Naphash Nachalah
shamamah Al Tannah
al Madbar
ky Adam amar
any hy rashash
han any ahy showb
aw banah charbah
Maqam kah amar al
Yachuwshauh al Tsaba cham
yash banah han ahy
harac aw cham
yash qara cham al
gabal al rashah
aw am al
Ashar Al Yachuwshauh
hayach zaam
Alam
aw Naphash ayn yash
raah aw yash amar
Al Yachuwshauh ahay huw
gadal al
gabal al yasharaAl
ban kabad Naphash
Ab aw abad
Naphash adan am az any
huw Ab ayah huw
any kabad aw am
any huw adan
ayah huw any Mara
Amar Al Yachuwshauh Al Tsaba
al attah La kahan
ky bazah any
sham aw attah amar

The burden of the word of the Lord 1
to Israel by Malachi.   1
I have love you,   2
said the Lord. yet
ye say, wherein
hast thou loved us?
was not Esau jacob's
bother? said the lord;
yet I loved jacob,   2
and I hated Esau,   3
and laid his mountains
and his heritage
waste for the dragons
of the wilderness.   3
whereas Edom saith,   4
we are impoverished,
but we will return
and build the desolate
places; thus saith the
Lord of hosts, they
shall build, but I will
throw down; and and they
shall call them, the
border of wickedness,
and the people against
whom the Lord
hath indignation
for ever.   4
and your eyes shall   5
see, and ye shall say,
The Lord will be
magnified from the
border of Israel.   5
a son honoureth his   6
father, and servant
his master; if then I
be a father, where is
mine honour? and if
I be a master,
where is my fear?
said the Lord of hosts
unto you, O priests,
that despise my
name. and ye say,

Mah hayach anachnw	wherein have we	
bazah yash sham	despised thy name?	6
attah Nagash gaal	ye offer polluted	7
Lacham al any Mazbaach	bread upon mine alter;	
aw attah amar Mah	and ye say, wherein	
hayach anachnw gaal attah	have we polluted thee?	
al ky attah amar al	In that ye say, the	
shalchan Al Yachuwshauh	table of the Lord	
huw bazah	is contemptible.	7
ky attah Nagash avvar al	if ye offer the blind for	8
zabach huw yash lah Ra	sacrifice, is it not evil?	
Aw ky attah Nagash al	and if ye offer the	
paccaach aw chalah huw yash lah	lame and sick, is it not	
Ra qarab yash Na ashar	evil? Offer it now unto	
attah pachah ahy huw	thy governor; will he	
ratsah ad attah	be pleased with thee,	
aw Nasa attah panym	or accept thy person?	
amar Al Yachuwshauh Tsaba	said the Lord of hosts.	8
aw attah Na	and now, I pray you,	9
chalah Al ky huw	beseech God that he	
ahy chanan al anachnw	will be gracious unto us:	
zath hayach arach Naphash	this hath been by your	
yad ahy huw Nasa	means: will he regard	
Naphash panym amar	your persons? Saith	
Al Yachuwshauh Al Tsaba	the Lord of hosts.	9
Mah huw sham gam	who is there even	10
al attah ky tsaba	among you that would	
cagar dalath al channam	shut the doors for naught?	
lah asah attah aR ash	neither do ye kindle fire	
al any Mazbaach al channam	on mine alter for naught.	
any hayach lah chaphats al attah	I have no pleasure in you,	
amar Al Yachuwshauh Al Tsaba	saith the Lord of hosts,	
lah ahy ratsah	neither will I accept	
ad Manchah al Naphash yad	an offering at your hand.	10
al al Mazrach al	for from the rising of the	11
shamash gam ashar al	sun even unto the	
Mabow al	going down of the	
huw any sham yash	same my name shall be	
gadal al gay	great among the Gentiles:	
aw al kal Maqam	and in every place	
qatar yash Nagash	incense shall be offered	
ashar any sham aw	unto my name, and	
Tahar Manchah al any	pure offering: for my	
sham yash gadal	name shall be great	
al gay	among the heathen,	
amar Al Yachuwshauh Al Tsaba	said the Lord of hosts.	11
han huw hayach chalal	but ye have profaned	12

yash al ky attah amar
al shalchan Al Yachuwshauh
huw gaal aw al

it, in that ye say,
The table of the Lord
is polluted and the

Nayb sham gam Naphash
akal huw bazah
attah amar gam hannah
Mah Mattalaah huw yash
aw attah hayach naphach
al yash amar Al Yachuwshauh Al Tsaba
aw attah bow ky
Asar hayach gazal aw
paccaach aw chalah
kah attah bow raa
Manchah yash
ratsah zath al Naphash
yad amar Al Yachuwshauh
han arar chava al
Nakal yash hayach
al Naphash adar zakar
aw Nadar aw
zabach al
Yachuwshauh shachath dabar
al any hayach gadal Malak
amar Al Yachuwshauh Al Tsaba
aw any sham huw
yara al
gay

fruit thereof, even his
meat, is contemptible.   12
ye said also, behold   13
what a weariness is it!
and ye have snuffed
at it, saith the Lord of hosts:
and ye brought that
which was torn, and
the lame, and the sick;
thus ye brought in
offering: should I
accept this of your
hand? saith the Lord.   13
But cursed be the   14
deceiver, which hath
in his flock a male,
and voweth, and
sacrificeth unto the
Lord a corrupt thing:
for I am a Great King,
saith the Lord of hosts,
and my name is
dreaadful among
the heathen.   14

chapter 2

aw attah la attah kahan	And now, O ye priests, 1
zath Matsavah huw	this commandment is
al attah	for you. 1
am attah ahy lah shama	if ye will not hear, 2
aw am attah ahy lah shwm	and if ye will not lay
yash lab Nathan kabad	it to heart, to give glory
ashar any sham amar	unto my name, saith
Al Yachuwshauh Al Tsaba	The Lord of hosts,
ahy gam shalach	I will even send a
Maarah al attah aw	curse upon you, and
ahy arar Naphash	I will curse your
Barakah gam any hayach	blessings: yea I have
arar cham kabar	curse them already,
ky attah asah lah	because ye do not
showm lab	lay it to heart. 2
han ahy gaar	Behold I will corrupt 3
Naphash zara aw zarah	your seed, and spread
parash al Naphash panym	dung upon your faces,
gam parash al	even the dung of
Naphash chag	your solemn feasts;
aw chash yash Nasa attah	and one shall take you
cuwr ad yash	away with it. 3
aw attah yash yada	And ye shall know 4
ky any hayach shalach zath	that I have sent this
Matsavah ashar attah	commandment unto you,
ky any Barath chayl	that my covenant might
kal zath Lava amar Al	be with levi saith the
Yachuwshauh Al Tsaba	Lord of hosts. 4
any Barath hayach han	My covenant was with 5
Naphash al chay aw shalam	him of life and peace;
aw Nathhan chamal Naphash	and I gave them to him
al al Mara ashar	for the fear where with
huw yara any aw hayach	he feared me, and was
chathath panym Naphash sham	afraid before my name. 5
Al Tarah al amath hayach	The law of truth was 6
al Naphash pah aw	in his mouth, and
aval hayach lah Matsa	iniquity was not found
al Naphash saphah huw halak	in his lips; he walked
han any al shalam aw	with me in peace and
Mayshar aw asah showb	equity; and did turn
rab cuwr al avan	many away from iniquity. 6
al al kahan saphah yash	for the priest's lips should 7
shamar daath aw cham	keep knowledge, and they
yash baqash al Tarah Al	should seek the Law at
Naphash pah al huw al	his mouth for; he is the

Malak Al Al Yachuwshauh Al Tsaba	Messenger of the Lord of hosts. 7
han attah huw cuwr	But ye are departed out 8
al al darak attah hayach Nathan	of the way, ye have caused
rab al kashal al Tarah	many to stumble at the law;
attah hayach shachath ky	ye have corrupted the
Baryath Al Lavay amar Al	covenant of levi saith the
Yachuwshauh Al Tsaba	Lord of hosts. 8
al hayach any gam Nathan	therefore hav I also made 9
attah bazah aw shaphal	you contemptible and base
panym kal al am pah	before all the people, according
huw attah hayach lah shamar any	as ye have not kept my
darak han hayach	ways but have been
Nasa al Al Tarah	partial in the law. 9
hayach anachnw lah kal achad Ab	have we not all one father? 10

yash lah achad Al bara anachnw	hath not one God created us?
Madda asah any asah bagad	why do we dealt treacherously
kal kash al Naphash	evey man against his
ach arach chalal al	brother by profaning the
Barayth al anachnw Ab	covenant of his father? 10
yachadah yash asah bagad	Judah hath dealt treacherously 11
aw ach Tabah huw	and an abomination is
asah al yasharaAl aw al	committed in Israel and in
shalam al yachadah yash	Jerusalem: for Judah hath
chalal al qadash ha Al	profaned the holiness of the
Yachuwshauh Asar huw ahab aw	Lord which he loved and
yash baal al bath	hath married the daughter
ha al Nakar Al	of a strange god. 11
Al Yachuwshauh ahy karath al kash	The Lord will cut off the man 12
ky asah zath al ar aw	that doeth this, the master and
al anah al al ky	the scholar out of the
ahal al yaaqab	tabernacles of Jacob, and
Naphash ky Nagash Manchah	him that offereth an offering
al Al Yachuwshauh Al Tsaba	unto the Lord of hosts. 12
aw zath hayach attah asah shany	and this have ye done again, 13
kacah al Mazbaach ha Al Yachuwshauh	covering the alter of the Lord
han damah han bakay aw	with tears with weeping, and
han anaqah bayth	with crying out insomuch
ky huw panah lah al	that he regardeth not the
Manchah kash ad aw laqach	offering any more or receiveth it
han ratsan ahy al Naphash yad	with good will at your hand 13
ad attah amar al al	yet ye say wherefore because 14
Al Yachuwshauh yash hayach ad	the Lord hath been witness
bayn attah aw al kashshah al	between thee and the wife of

attah Naar al Asar
yash asah bagad
ad huw Naphash attah chabarath
aw al kashshah al attah barayth
aw asah lah huw asah achad
ad hayach huw al shaar al al
ruwach aw Mah achad
Ky huw chayl baqash Alasham
zara kan Nasa shamar
al Naphash ruwach aw yanach al
asah bagad al
al kashshsh al Naphash Naar
al Al yachuwshauh al Alasham al yasharaAl
amar ky huw sana shalach
cuwr al achad kacah
ach han Naphash labash amar
Al Yachuwshauh Al Tsaba kan
Nasa shamar al Naphash ruwach ky

thy youth against whom
thou hast dealt treacherously:
yet is she thy companion
and the wife of thy covenant   14
and did not he make one?   15
ye had he the residue of the
spirit and wherefore one?
that he might seek a godly
seed therefor take heed
to your spirit and let none
deal treacherously aganist
the wife of his youth   15
for the Lord the God of Israel,   16
saith that he hateth putting
away; for one covereth
violence with his garment saith
the Lord of host. Therefore
take heed to your spirit that

attah asah lah bagad
attah hayach yaga Al Yachuwshauh
han Naphash dabar ad attah amar
Mah hayach any yaga
Naphash yowm attah amar kal
achad ky asah ra huw
Tab al al ayn ha Al Yachuwshauh
aw huw chaphats al cham
aw ayach huw Al Alasham al Mashpat

ye deal not treacherously   16
ye have wearied the Lord   17
with your words yet ye say
wherein have we wearied
him? when ye say every
one that doeth evil is
good in the sight of the Lord
and he delighteth in them
or where is the God of Judgment 17

chapter 3

han ahy shalach any
Malak aw yash
panah al darak panym any
aw Al Yachuwshauh Asar attah baqash
yash patham bow al Naphash
haykal gam al Malak al
al barayth Asar attah
chahats al hannah huw yash
bow amar Al Yachuwshauh Al Tsaba
han my wlay kwl al yowm
al Naphash bow aw my yash
amad yowm huw raah
al huw kamw Tsaraph ash

Behold I will send my   1
Messenger, and he shall
prepare the way before me:
and the Lord, whom ye seek,
shall suddenly come to his
temple, even the Messenger of
the covenant, whom ye
delight in: behold, he shall
come, saith the Lord of hosts.   1
But who may abide the day   2
of his coming? And who shall
stand when he appeareth?
for he is like a refiner's fire,

aw kamw kahac Barayth	and like fuller's soap	2
aw yash yashab huw Tsaraph	and hw shall sit as a refiner	3
aw tahar al kacaph aw huw	and purifier of silver and he	
yash tahar al ban al Lavay	shall purify the sons of levi	
aw zaqaq cham huw zahab aw	and purge them as gold and	
kacaph ky cham wlay Nagash	silver that they may offer	
al Al Yachuwshauh Manchah	unto the Lord an offering	
al Tsadaqah	in righteousness	3
az yash al Manchah al	Then shall the offering of	4
yachadah aw shalam arab	Judah and Jersalem be pleasant	
ashar Al Yachuwshauh huw al yowm	unto the Lord as in the days	
al Alam aw al qadmany shanah	of old, and as in former years.	4
aw ahy qarab attah	and I will come near to you	5
Mashpat aw ahy	to Judgment: and I will be a	
Mahar ad al al	swift witness against the	
kashaph aw al al	sorcerers, and against the	
Naaph aw al	adulterers, and against	
shaqar shaba aw al	false swearers, and against	
cham ky ashaq al	those that oppress the	
sakyr al Naphash sakar al	hireling in his wages, the	
almanah aw al yatham	widow, and the fatherless,	
aw ky Natah al	and that turn aside the	
gar al Naphash yaman	stranger from his right	
aw yara lah any amar Al	and fear not me. saith the	
Yachuwshauh Al Tsaba	Lord of hosts.	5
al hayach Al Yachuwshauh any shanah	For I am the Lord, I change	6
lah kan attah ban al	not: therefore ye sons of	
yaaqab huw lah kalah	Jacob are not consumed.	6
gam al al yowm al Naphash	even from the days of your	7
Ab attah huw cuwr	fathers ye are gone away	
al any chaq aw	from mine ordinances, and	
hayach lah shamar cham shuwb	have not kept them. return	
al any and ahy showb	unto me, and I will return	
al attah amar Al Yachuwshauh Al	unto you, saith the Lord of	
Tsaba han attah amar Mah	hosts. But ye said, wherein	
yash any shuwb	shall we return?	7
ahy adam qaba Alasham ad	will a man rob God? Yet	8
attah hayach qaba any han	ye have robbed me. but	
attah amar Mah hayach	ye say wherein have	
any qaba attah al	we robbed thee?	
Maasah aw Taramah	tithes and offerings.	8
attah huw arar han Maarah	ye are cursed with a curse:	9
al attah hayach qaba any	for ye have robbed me,	
gam zath kal gay	even this hold nation.	9
bow attah kal al Maasar	bring ye all the tithes	10
al al wtsar ky	into the storehouse, that	
sham wlay huw Taraph al any	there may be meat in mine	
bayth aw bachan any Na	house, and prove me now	
zath amar Al Yachuwshauh	herewith, saith the Lord	

Al Tsaba am ahy lah
pathach attah al arabbah al
shamaym aw shachaph attah
Barakahy sham
yash lah rachab day
laqach yash
aw ahy gaar al
akal al Naphash dabrah
aw huw yash lah shachath
al paray al Naphash adamah
lah yash Naphash gaphan
shakal Naphash sakal panym Al
ath sadah amar Al
Yachuwshauh Al Tsaba
aw kal gay yash Asar attah
ashar al yash
chaphats arats amar
Al Yachuwshauh Al Tsaba
Naphash dabar hayach chazaqm Al
al any amar Al Yachuwshauh
ad attah amar Mah hayach
any dabar kan rabah
 al attah
attah hayach amar yash shav
abad Alasham aw Mah
batsa yash ky any hayach
Shamar Naphash MaShmarath
ky any hayach halak
qadarannyth panym Al
Yachuwshauh Al Tsaba
aw attah any Asar al
zad shalah gam cham
ky asah rashah
huw banah gam cham
ky bachan Alasham huw gam
Malat
az cham ky yara
Al Yachuwshauh dabar day achad
Al raa aw Al
Yachuwshauh qashab aw
shama aw caphar
Al zakar hayach
kathab panym Naphash al
cham ky yara Al
Yachuwshauh aw ky chashab
al Naphash sham
aw cham yash any
amar Al Yachuwshauh Al Tsaba al
ky yowm ashar any asah

of hosts, if I will not
open you the windows of
heaven, and pour you out
a blessing, that there
shall not be room enough
to receive it. 10
and I will rebuke the 11
devourer for your sakes,
and he shall not destroy
the fruits of your ground:
Neither shall your vine
cast her fruit before the
time in the field, saith the
Lord of hosts. 11
and all nations shall call you 12
blessed: for ye shall be a
delightsome land, said
The Lord of hosts. 12
your words have been stout 13
against me, saith the Lord.
yet ye say, what have
we spoken so much
against thee? 13
ye have said, It is vain 14
to serve God: and what
profit is it that we have
kept his ordinance, and
that we have walked
mournfully before the
Lord of hosts? 14
and now we call the 15
proud happy yea they
that work wickness
are set up yea they
that tempt God are even
delivered 15
then they that feared 16
the Lord spake often one
to another and the
Lord hearkened and
heard it and a book
of remembrance was
written before him for
them that feared the
Lord and that thought
upon his name 16
and they shall be mine 17
saith the Lord of hosts, in
that day when I make

al any cagallah aw ahy
chamal cham huw kash
chamal Naphash ratsan ban
ky abad Naphash
az yash shuwb
aw raah bayn al
Tsaddyq aw al rasha
bayn Naphash ky abad
Alasham aw Naphash ky abad
Naphash lah

up my Jewel's and I will
spare them as a man
spareth his own son
that serveth him 17
then shall ye return 18
and discern between the
righteousness and the wicked,
between him that serveth
God and him that serveth
him not. 18

chapter 4

al hannah al yowm bow
ky yash baar huw ach
Tannar aw kal azad
gam aw kal ky asah
rashah yash qash
aw al yowm ky bow
yash lahat cham
amar Al Yachuwshauh Al Tsaba
ky yash azab cham
lah sharash aw anaph
han ashar attah yara
any sham yash al shamash
Al Tsadaqah zarach
han Marpa al Naphash kanaph
aw yash yatsa aw
pash huw agal
al al Marbaq
aw yash acac
al rasha al cham
yash aphar tachath al
kaph al Naphash ragal al
yowm ky yash asah zath
amar Al Yachuwshauh Al Tsaba
zakar attah Al Tarah
Al Mashash any abad
ashar any Tsavah al
Naphash al charab al kal
yasharaAl han al chaq
aw Mashpat
hannah ahy shalach attah
Alayachuw al Naby panym
al bow al gadal
aw yara yowm al
Al Yachuwshauh

For, behold the day cometh, 1
that shall burn as an
oven: and all the proud,
yea, and all that do
wickedly, shall be stubble:
and the day that cometh
shall burn them up,
saith the Lord of hosts
that it shall leave them
neither root nor branch. 1
But unto you that fear 2
my name shall the sun
of righteousness arise
with healing in his wings;
and ye shall go forth, and
grow up as calves
of the stall. 2
and ye shall tread down 3
the wicked: for they
shall be ashes under the
soles of your feet in the
day that I shall do this,
saith the Lord of hosts. 3
remember ye the law 4
of Moses my servant,
which I commanded unto
him in Horeb for all
Israel, with the statutes
and Judgments. 4
Behold I will send you 5
Elijah the prophet before
the coming of the great
and dreadful day of
the Lord: 5

aw yash shuwb al
lab al Ab al
ban aw al lab al
al ban al cham
Ab pan any bow aw
Nakah al arats han charam

and he shall turn the   6
heart of the fathers to the
children, and the heart of
the children to their
fathers, lest I come and
smite the earth with a curse.   6

ⴵ א	Aleph	aw-Lef
⊂ ⊃	Beyth	
⅂ ⅂	Daleth	daw-leth
Ⴖ	he	hay
|ⴄL	Vav	
|⟨	Zayin	
Ⴖ	Chevth	
⅂ ⅂	Yowde	
⅃ ⅂	Kaph	caf
⅃ ⟩	Lamed	Law med
ⴵ □	Mem	mame
⅃	NuWN	Noon
▽ ▽	Camek	Saw mck
Y Ɏ	AYiN	ah-YiN
⅃ ⟩	phe	fay
Ƴ	Tsadev	
⅁	Qowph	Cofe
⅁ ⟨	Revsh	
ⴵ ⴵ	shivn	sheen
Ⴠ Ⴠ	Thav	

chapter 1

1.al the
2.Massa burden
3.al of
4.dabar the word
5.al the
6.Yachuwshauh Lord
7.al to
8.yasharaAl Israel
9.arach by
10.Malachy Malachi
11.any I
12.hayach have
13. ahab loved
14.attah you
15.attah said
16.al the
17.ad yet
18.attah ye
19.amar say
20.Mah wherein
21.yash hast thou
22.anachnw us
23.lah not
24.rash Esau
25.yaaqab Jacob
26.ah brother
27.sana hated
28.aw and
29.shuwm laid
30.Naphash his
31.har mountains
32.Nachalah heritage
33.shamamah waste
34.Tannah dragons
35.Madbar wilderness
36.ky whereas
37.adam Edom
38.rashash impoverished

39.han but
40.any we
41.ahy will
42.shuwb return
43.banah build
44.charbah desolate
45.Maqam places
46.kah thus
47.Tsaba hosts
48.cham they
49.harac throw down
50.qara call
51.cham them
52.gabal border
53.al of
54.rashah wickedness
55.am people
56.al against
57.Asar whom
58.hayach hath
59.zaam indignation
60.alam for ever
61.Naphash your
62.ayn eyes
63.raah see
64.gabal magnified
65.ban son
66.kabad honoreth
67.Ab father
68.abad servant
69.adan master
70.am if
71.az then
72.huw be
73.ayah where
74.any mine
75.huw is
76.any my
77.Mara fear
78.al unto
79.la O
80.kahan priest
81.ky that
82.bazah despise
83.sham name
84.aw and
85.attah ye
86.Nagash offer
87.gaal polluted

88.lacham bread
89.al upon
90.Mazbaach altar
91.shalchan table
92.bazah contemptible
93.avvar blind
94.zabach sacrifice
95.huw is
96.yash it
97.lah not
98.ra evil
99.paccaach lame
100.chalah sick
101.pachah governor
102.ratsah be pleased
103.aw or
104.Nasa accept
105.panym person
106.Na I pray you
107.chalah beseech
108.ahy will be
109.chanan gracious
110.zath this
111.hayach hath been
112.yad means
113.Nasa regard
114.cagar shut
115.dalath the doors
116.qarab offer
117.sham there
118.gam even
119.Tsaba would
120.channam naught
121.asah do
123.ar kindle
124.ash fire
125.chaphats pleasure
126.Mazrach rising
127.shamash sun
128.Mabow going down
129.huw same
130.yash shall be
131.gadal great
132.gay Gentiles
133.qatar incense
134.Tahar pure
135.chalal profaned
136.akal meat
137.Mattalaah weariness

138.Naphach snuffed
139.hayach which
140.gazal torn
141.han but
142.arar cursed
143.Nakal deceiver
144.adar flock
145.zakar male
146.Nadar voweth
147.zabach sacrificeth
148.Malak king
149.yara dreadful

chapter 2

150.Matsavah commandment
152.al for
153.shama hear
154.shuwm lay
155.Nathan to give
156.kabad glory
157.shalach sent
158.Maarah curse
159.arar curse
160.barakah blessings
161.kabar already
162.ky because
163.gaar corrupt
164.zara seed
165.zarah spead
166.parash dung
167.panym faces
168.chag solemn feasts
169.shuwm lay it
170.kash one
171.Nasa take
172.cuwr away
173.yada know
174.ashar unto
175.barayth covenant

176.chayl might
177.lavay levi
178.amar saith
179.chay life
180.shalam peace
181.Nathan I gave
182.Mara fear
183.Asar wherewith
184.yara feared
185.any me
186.chathath afraid
187.Tarah law
188.amath truth
189.aval iniquity
190.Matsa found
191.saphah lips
192.Mayshar equity
193.shuwb turn
194.rab many
195.avan iniquity
196.shamar keep
197.daath knowledge
198.baqash seek
199.pah mouth
200.Malak messenger
201.huw are
202.cuwr depated out
203.darak way
204.kashal stumble
205.shamar kept
206.Nasa partial
207.kal all
208.achad one
209.yash hath
210.Al God
211.bara created
212.Madda why
213.asah deal
214.bagad treacherously
215.al against
216.ach brother
216.arach by
217.chalal profaning
218.anachnw our
219.yachadah Judah
220.baal married
221.qadash holiness
222.bath daughter
223.Nakar strange

224.al god
225.karath cut off
226.ar master
227.anah scholar
228.ahal tabernacles
229.Manchah offering
230.shany again
231.kacah covering
232.damah tears
233.bakay
234.anaqah crying out
235.bayth insomuch
236.hayach been
237.ad witness
238.bayn between
239.kashshah wife
240.Naar youth
241.chabarath companion
242.shaar residue
243.ruwach spirit
244.baqash might
245.Alasham godly
246.yanach let
247.yasharaAl Israel
248.shalach putting
249.labash garment
250.kan therefore
251.dabar words
252.yaga wearied
253.ra evil
254.Tab good
255.ayn sight
256.yowm when
257.amar say
258.chaphats delighteth
259.ayah where
260.Mashpat Judgment

chapter 3

261.han behold
262.panah prepare
263.patham suddenly
264.haykal temple
265.kowl abide
266.amad stand
267.raah appeareth
268.kamw like
269.Tsaraph refiner's
270.ash fire
271.kabac fullers
272.boryth soap
273.Tahar purify
274.zaqaq purge
275.zahab gold
276.kacaph silver
277.Tsadaqah in righteousness
278.arab be pleasant
279.alam old
280.qadman former
281.shanah years
282.ahy I will
283.qarab come near
284.Mahar
285.kashaph sorcerers
286.Naaph adulterers
287.shaqar false
288.shaba swearers
289.ashaq oppress
290.sakyr hireling
291.sakar wages
292.almanah window
293.yatham fatherless
294.Natah turn aside
295.gar stranger
296.yamyn right
297.chaq ordinances
298.qaba rob

299.bow bring
300.Maasar
301.wtsar storehouse
302.bachan prove
303.Na now
304.zath herewith
305.pathach open
306.rachab room
307.laqach to receive
308.yash it
309.paray fruits
310.adamah ground
311.gaphan vine
312.shakal cast
313.sadah field
314.gay nations
315.Asar call
316.chazaq stout
317.shav vain
318.abad to serve
319.batsa profit
320.Mashmarath ordinance
321.halak walked
322.qadarannyth mournfully
323.zad proud
324.shalah happy
325.huw are
326.banah set up
327.gam even
328.Malat delivered
329.qashab hearkened
330.caphar book331.
332.zakar remembrance
333.kathab written
334.chashab thought
334.cagallah jewels
335.kash man
336.ban son
337.raah discern
338.rasha the wicked

chapter 4

339.hannah behold
340.baar burn
341.Tannar oven
342.azad the proud
343.rashah wicked
344.qash stubble
345.lahat burn up
346.azab leave
347.cham them
348.sharash root
349.anaph branch
350.zarach arise
351.Marpa healing
352.kanaph wings
353.yatsa go forth
354.pash grow up
355.huw as
356.agal calves
357.Marbaq stall
358.acac tread down
359.aphar ashes
360.Tachath under
361.kaph soles
362.ragal feet
363.Mashash Moses
364.Tsavah
365.charab Horeb
366.Alayachuwshauh Elijah
367.yowm day
368.arats the earth
369.charam a curse